ALL THE WEB'S A STAGE

HOW TO MAKE YOUR BUSINESS A HIT ON THE INTERNET BY MICHELLE KABELE

IDEASTORM PRESS

ISBN 9780982068625

Library of Congress Control Number: 2008936459

TABLE OF CONTENTS

OPENING CREDITS

Show me the money! **(JERRY MAGUIRE)**

If you're feeling a little "Jerry Maguire-like" when it comes to conducting business on the Internet, believe me, you're not alone. Harnessed correctly and strategically, the Web becomes an amazing stage for not only brand awareness but also for profitability with direct results landing on your bottom line. The Internet is a powerful tool if you understand how it works, what you can expect from doing business online, and how to make the most of all the resources available to you.

At the core of the Internet lies hundreds of thousands of websites. So how do you get your website noticed? How do you cut through all the clutter, create a website rich with pertinent yet interesting content that summons Google's GoogleBot crawler? How do you make it to the top of the search engine's list with five out of five stars, ranking number one on the search engine's first page? Think of your website as the production stage. It's where you tell your story, with each page showcasing a unique part of your business. Your website may garner great reviews or be lost on page 10 of a Google search. But if you remember that your company has control over the final performance, you'll find yourself on the channel partner's version of the Hollywood Walk of Fame not long after your premiere.

In this book, I'll be talking about the debut of the World Wide Web in 1989, when producers first came on the scene using a web browser to view text, images, videos, and more, and then navigated from website to website using hyperlinks. These forerunners originally thought they could use the Internet to share – worldwide – publicly accessible information. But as more and more people realized that the Internet could be used for so much more in many different ways, the Web soon evolved into a source of not just information, but income as well. Behind the scenes, business owners and channel partnerss like you quickly realized the untapped potential of the Internet.

BE UNIQUE AND STRAIGHT-FORWARD

Many channel partners think that creating a great presence on the Web is simply creating a website like that of the competition. However, enter the critics, those high-ranking search engines like Google, Yahoo!, MSN, and others, who literally control who soars and who flops. Search engines do have a soft spot, however, and they offer insider tips to designing your website from the inside out in order to garner top rankings. I'll show you how search engines work and what you can do to manipulate them.

DON'T SHOW YOUR AGE

You may not quite know exactly who is looking at you, but social networks and user-generated content on the Web are all the rage – and not just for kids. Places like MySpace, Facebook, YouTube, and personal blogs are working their way into email threads, finding their way into shopping carts; even folks like Brian Williams, Donald Trump and Kirstie Alley have active blogs and are jumping in on these latest trends. Don't get caught on the downward slope of the technology curve. These peak spots are useful tools for businesses, too, and you run the risk of falling behind the competition if you just brush them off as teenage fun.

WHAT IS YOUR ULTIMATE GOAL?

What do you want from the Web? What do you expect to gain here? And what's in it for your viewers? How do you gain a captive audience? Your story is written but now how do you build each scene? What is your message and how do you want visitors to respond? Do you want them to simply find you and use you as a resource for information? Or do you want your audience to click-through to your shopping cart and return time and time again? One of the most critical missteps in creating a high-ranking presence on the Web is building a website without first thinking through the process in which you want your visitor to experience.

Once you know what you want your audience to experience, you need to determine what they want to encounter while viewing your website as well. Do you have a great story to tell? Does your story make you memorable and does it communicate your value proposition? There are all sorts of ways to keep your audience engaged in your site and I'll share some simple ideas that will help your bottom line.

Lastly, how will a search engine know you exist? Through SEO, or search engine optimization. We'll talk about what it is, why you need it and why it's critical to incorporate keywords and title tags before you start creating your website. Critics always provide great analysis in their reviews and we'll take a look at some free analytical programs that can help you decide what works for your site and what needs to be reworked to make your site perform better.

"May the force be with you." **(STAR WARS)**

No, you don't have to be Luke Skywalker and take on the Dark Side. But you will need a strategic plan to conquer the complexities of the Internet – and a way to devise a plan that is clear, concise, and ultimately award winning. Grab your bucket of popcorn and 32-ounce Coke. It's showtime, folks.

ACT ONE ■ Setting the Scene: The Wonders of the Web

"It's alive! It's alive!" **(FRANKENSTEIN)**

Just 20 years ago, who knew that a technology would come at us so fast and furious that we now live and breathe it? Like air and water – we can't live without it. Technological advances progressed so rapidly that we were playing catch up before we even knew we were falling behind. The Web was alive and breathing.

When the World Wide Web debuted in 1989 as an off-shoot of the Internet, it was a giant experiment, a global theory that was originally created to be a part of military strategy and not meant for private use. The Internet, which is what the Web is laid down upon, actually started in the 1950s as an experiment by the Department of Defense. They wanted to come up with something that would enable secure communications between various military units. Private technology quickly landed in the public eye. Once news of this new technology spread, it kept feeding off itself. Universities such as Harvard and Berkeley learned of this new technology and made important modifications to it, and the World Wide Web grew and grew.

Today, more than 600 million people have access to the Web. They use it for research (like I did for this chapter to learn more about the history of this beast), for exchanging information, for keeping up with the latest in local, national and world news, for shopping, for business, and ultimately for building relationships between so many different facets of life.

And how much do you think the Internet and Web affect you? Let me ask you this: "Can you go a whole day without checking your email?" "What would happen if you couldn't read your headline news online today?" "When you're bored at work, do you grab your mouse and keyboard and do a little surfing?" (It's O.K., I won't tell.) Try going camping for a weekend in the woods. Would you be relaxed that you're away from your computer or stressed because you didn't have access to the Internet? What has this incredible technology done to us?

"Mama always said, 'Life was like a box of chocolates; you never know what you're gonna get.'" **(FORREST GUMP)**

At the root of the Web is this: you truly don't always know what you're going to get. At its simplest, the Web is a tool to communicate and to do so globally through a web browser that allows us to view text, images, videos, and more, and then navigate from website to website using hyperlinks. It's an adventure on the technological highway – and chances are you're going way over the speed limit.

But with more and more people realizing that the Internet can be used for so much more in many different ways, the Web continues to evolve into a source of not just information, but income as well. People use it to check the up-to-the-minute weather in their local area – hourly. A wine connoisseur who lives in Omaha can order the finest wines from France with the click of a mouse. And she can do it in her pajamas!

"In bed by nine? That's when life just begins."

(GENTLEMEN PREFER BLONDES)

That's right, thanks to the Web, your business can now be open 24 hours a day, seven days a week, 365 days year – and it is, when you have a website. The Web is a huge stage for you to show off your business, literally, to the world. No longer are your customers just local or regional. You now have the potential to work with customers and provide products and services to other businesses halfway around the world. Of course, how you present yourself is up to you.

Since technically your website is "live" all the time, you must decide what your message is. What do you want to communicate to your customers and potential customers? Will a future customer in New Delhi be able to order something at 1 p.m. his time and still receive your products in a timely manner? What if a customer in Vienna needs technical support at 10 a.m. her time? Are you still in throes of R.E.M. sleep on the East Coast? Now you must anticipate your customers' needs, regardless of their location in the world. Remember, how you perform on the Web's stage is up to you. Write your script carefully and anticipate every need and crisis that may occur.

ACT TWO ■ Search Engines: Bad Guys or Heroes?

"I'm not bad. I'm just drawn that way." **(ROGER RABBIT)**

Search engines own you. They may not control how you look on the Web, but they wield the power of online success.

Let me explain. You can have the glitziest website out there. Upon entering your site, your visitor may be dazzled by a beautiful Flash intro, with an audio stream of your voice welcoming the visitor to learn more. Great! This is your "Taaa Daaa Moment". The problem? Search engines won't see it – and it most likely won't register as the tiniest blip on their radar when they come searching to rank you in their search engine.

While there are many search engines out there, the top three – Google, Yahoo! and MSN – are the Big Three, the ones you'll want to focus on. These are the most popular — and therefore powerful — engines. They are most likely the ones that could decide whether your online business soars or flops. It's more than just "throwing up a website" and crossing your fingers. You need to maximize this potent marketing tool by completely understanding how search engines tick. Here in lies the secret to successful Web presence.

There are two types of search engines – crawlers and human-based directories. Crawlers find your site, read through it, and then rank it within their engine. Your hope? That someone searches for your product or service and your business shows up on the first page, or better yet the top five, of the results the search engine provides. Human-powered directories are a bit different. They are Open Directories, which means they require a human to update it. Crawlers are the most common and used by the Big Three.

So here's a quick picture of how Google, Yahoo! and MSN search engines work. First the crawler, also known as the spider, visits your homepage, reads it, and then follows links to other pages within your site. The spider returns to the site on a regular basis, such as every month or two, to look for changes. This is why you want to keep your content fresh. Yes, it's great to keep new ideas flowing for customers who keep coming back to your site, but it's also important to the search engines. The crawlers look for new content to prove that your site is "active."

Then, everything the spider finds goes into an index. The index is like a giant book containing a copy of every web page that the spider finds. If a web page changes, then this book is updated with new information. Sometimes it can take a while for new pages or changes that the spider finds to be added to the index. Until your site is indexed it won't show up in a search. Finally search engine software sifts through the millions of pages recorded in the index to find matches to a search and rank them in order of what it believes is most relevant for what that person was looking for.

As you design your site, remember that these crawlers can only read text, not graphics. So, while your designer may have created a slick website, if your keywords don't appear in text format, the crawlers can't rank your site. To check, try to highlight the text and copy it. If you can do this, it's designed using text. If you can click and drag the area, while it may look like text, it's actually a graphic. Have your webmaster change this imme- diately to text so crawlers can see you! Lastly, create a site map of your site and put a table of contents on your server. This will also help in your rankings. A great website to learn more about site maps is www.sitemaps.org.

As you develop your site, take a look at Google's webmaster tools, yet another free way to get tips on creating a search engine-friendly site. Continually updating your site and refreshing your content will also keep you highly ranked.

ACT THREE ■ Web 2.0, The Sequel

"A martini. Shaken, not stirred." (GOLDFINGER)

You never quite know whom you're going to meet at a cocktail party. Or a book club meeting. Or even a family picnic for that matter (could be Nana Jane's long-lost cousin who becomes your next biggest customer). You carry your business cards with you religiously and hand them out when appropriate. Socializing on the Web is no different. You never know whom you might stumble across. Your next customer may come from some online location you never expected.

Today, social networking online allows you to electronically build (and maintain) a community of friends, family members, and colleagues. Don't stick up your nose and dismiss websites like MySpace, Facebook, and LinkedIn as just for kids or only for fun in your spare time (do you even have any of that?). The Web 2.0 world is transforming how you execute your business-to-business marketing plan. Blogs, podcasts, RSS feeds, videocasts, wikis, and social networks and communities are all tools being used, equally, to reach both prospects and existing customers.

Recent surveys show that marketing budgets have shrunk, yet small businesses believe in Web 2.0 enough to spend the limited dollars they do have in this area. These online social networks, or "webs," grow from conversations among people who share a common affinity. For instance, members of an online community might all work for the same company or in the same industry. They could share the same interests in a common thread or idea. But, these like-minded people may differ in other ways, such as their locations, "office" hours, industries, or employers. So, when

15

all these folks want to hold a discussion, they can now have conversations online through these social networks, breaking down the barriers that their differences may have caused in the past. Imagine if you could get all of your end-users in a room and ask them, "what do you need and how can I make your life better?" That's exactly what Web 2.0 can deliver, in a virtual room.

FACEBOOK: IT'S NOT JUST FOR KIDS!

Just look at some of the benefits of Facebook. This online community was launched in 2004 as a means for connecting Harvard students. The site grew to connect students from other college campuses and eventually welcomed anyone aged 13 or older. At present, more than 62 million people connect via Facebook — and I guarantee that there's a lot of business going on here!

You can use Facebook as a great resource to generate awareness for your brand. First, you need to recognize that changing face of today's consumers. Gone are the folks who want prices and specs. With the onslaught of easily accessible information, consumers now want "relationships". They desire personal connections with those they choose to do business with. So the idea of social media is a perfect fit in your marketing strategy because it brings you into the all-important relationship component that is likely missing from your mix.

Facebook has become increasingly popular with professionals and can be a cross-point for building relationships with both existing customers and new prospects. You can use your page on this site to communicate promotions, contests and events, share knowledge, raise awareness of your business' offerings, and also drive traffic directly to your website. This forum allows you to not just wait to find out what customers are saying and seeking, but brings you into the conversation! You can post your ideas and your solutions and become a valuable resource. Suddenly your e-friend community grows as word spreads. This social networking is an R&D specialist's dream! You can use it as your "test kitchen" for new ideas! And, if you've ever wondered what others are saying about you, your brand or your business, you'll learn it here through actual product users.

Your Facebook profile will also boost your organic search engine results. The ongoing activity on your page does not escape the watchful eye of search engines' spiders that are seeking active, up-to-date content.

Of course, you'll find plenty of opportunities to find new customers in areas and categories you may never have thought of with traditional marketing, and it can also be used as a lead generation tool to help you qualify potential customers who you can best serve.

INDIRECT MARKETING

Think of Facebook, and all the social media, as "indirect mail". Rather than buying lists of names that match your demographic and pursue them directly, Web 2.0 brings people to you so that you can then share your message with them. Your audience is lining up, all prepared to hear what you have to say because they've been brought to your page on the recommendation of their friends. That's how it works. In the world of Web 2.0, you make "friend requests" when you want to get to know someone. The more friends you have out there, the greater your reach into more networks. This approach takes "word of mouth" to a whole new level!

By now you know that having a corporate online presence for your business is critical. You've probably built your website and are looking for ways to increase your company's visibility, improve sales, attract new customers, and be the information resource for your existing customers. Many of these online social networks seem like they are personal networks. Karen is talking to her brother John about her four-year-old's Monet masterpiece. John's friend, Charlie, chimes in and says he wants to see a copy of the photo because he knows a local art dealer who specializes in paintings done by talented young amateurs. Can you see where this conversation is headed? A simple personal conversation can lead anywhere – just like an off-the-cuff chat at a holiday party or Rotary Club meeting. But, with social networks, your reach has no limits!

MySpace is another cool tool that enables you to proactively create a chain of events like the one above. It's an online communication service that uses a combination of email, photos, weblogs, forums, and user profiles. You can network in your own style and on your own time – and it's free.

Linkedin is another digital networking tool with over 21 million users, and every Fortune 500 company is listed/represented on Linkedin. These electronic tools provide outstanding 24/7 personal references.

GET STARTED.

How can you use these powerful tools?

1. **First you have to have a profile.** You can set up your page quickly, using templates. Then search the network to identify and communicate with people within the network.

2. **Prospect:** You may be surprised at how many people you know and/or can reach using this networking tool. Remember the phrase "a friend of a friend"? You're more likely to get a response to your inquiry using this tool – especially if you have referrals and/or are connected through the network. On Linked in, use the "get connected" or "get introduced" to "meet" another member.

3. **Thought Leadership:** Many of these tools now offer a Q+A section where you can seek help from other members. Conversely, you can provide answers and insights that show-case your expertise. When other members can search these topics, they get linked to your profile and immediately see that you are someone they want to connect with!

4. **Referrals:** Members can recommend other members, which acts as an "endorsement" that others can see when they review your profile. Leverage your newfound friendships and your network will grow quickly.

5. **Search Engine Optimization (SEO):** Your complete profile will come up in searches using Google, Yahoo, MSN, or other search engines. When you have populated your content as I mentioned above, these networks can be powerful marketing tools that support your business objectives.

6. **User Groups:** Organizations can create "groups" where members who have a common interest or goal are linked together. This feature makes finding contacts with similar interests fast and easy. Starting a user group is just as simple. You can even use your logo as the user group icon — a nice brand-building bonus!

Best of all, these are free tools you can use today, just by logging in and spending a little time managing your digital profile. If you're looking for a smart investment of your time, you'll get amazing ROI here!

Once you establish your own profile, contact your friends, family, and colleagues and encourage them to visit you and create profiles of their own. And the networking — and the fun — begins. Soon, your friend told a friend about your great new product, and they chimed in and were interested in learning more. It's the trickle effect. It's Six Degrees of Kevin Bacon! Right now, there are more than 55 million MySpace members— two and a half times the amount of traffic as Google—and the site is ranked as the seventh most popular English language website. With that many potential folks joining your community, you just never know whom you might end up linked to. And, like Facebook, you can integrate your personal connections with your business connections by driving traffic to your website, building awareness for your business, and talking about new promotions, events, and contests.

These are some simple ways to use social networking in your business right now. Just make sure you refresh your content often to stay relevant and compelling so you maintain your readers and their interest. Because social networking is dynamic, it will keep changing, and probably quickly, if past history of the World Wide Web is any indication. But it's a great way to begin to build a following for your business or product, and everyone is using it.

ACT FOUR ■ Get Great Reviews with E-news

"Someday you'll learn that greatness is only the seizing of opportunity - clutching with your bare hands 'til the knuckles show white." **(NATIONAL VELVET)**

Keeping with our focus of seizing every opportunity to communicate with your customers through your website, offer up some value-added goodies (how about a free soda with that popcorn?), and position yourself as the Super channel partner with all the answers (or at least the network of resources to solve your customers' problems). While we've talked about how to tell (and sell) your story throughout your website, what about creating a preview of great things to come? How can you entice new and existing customers to enter your site?

Taadaa! Introducing the e-newsletter.

"What we've got here is a failure to communicate." **(COOL HAND LUKE)**

One of the most strategic methods of marketing communications today (and one of the least expensive and easiest to do) is the e-newsletter. Like their paper predecessors, they communicate news and information to a targeted group of recipients who can benefit from this knowledge. The benefits of e-news are vast:

- Increase awareness and build recognition for your brand.

- Position yourself and your company as a leader and resource in the industry.

- Provide timely and informative tips to your existing customers who rely on your insight to fix their problems.

- Alert existing and potential customers to trends in the industry, keeping them ahead of the competition.

- Gain a higher response rate to your information or deals simply because you're targeting a specific, receptive audience.

- Capture critical customer data and information that will help you better focus future sales and marketing plans.

- Creates a means to track your efforts and see the results (that all important ROI) – or tweak your plans to make them work even better!

AND

- E-newsletters are a cost-effective and effective way to maintain ongoing communications with your customers.

"You're gonna need a bigger boat." (JAWS)

What's so fantastic about e-newsletters is that they work in tandem with your website. Your e-news should be filled with links to your site, creating one portal after another to land them squarely in a front row seat to your stage! Once you get them in there and they discover that you are a powerhouse of great stuff, they'll spread the word to others. An e-newsletter that offers up trendy news and information will be passed along from email recipient to email recipient. It's the viral effect we all love. Your core customer database will spread your word for you and you don't even have to ask them to do it!

Think about all the e-newsletters you opt in to or out of on a daily basis. I can't think of the last time that I went to a website where there wasn't some sort of newsletter sign-up button grabbing my attention. If the topic is something that piques your interest, you click. And, you know that you can always unsubscribe, so it's a no-brainer. The job of keeping you engaged as a subscriber is the responsibility of the e-news editor.

"Life is a banquet, and most poor suckers are starving to death!" **(AUNTIE MAME)**

As you begin to think about what to say, and promote, to your customers, develop two themes in your mind:

1. What you think your customers might want to know; and
2. What you want your customers to buy in to.

For instance, your customer needs to sell 15,000 widgets to his customers, but he's not quite sure how to ship them once the sale is complete. In your e-newsletter, you may serve up a remedy to this kind of situation, which will help your customers and make you look like the Super channel partner for solving their problems! At the same time, you may also be able to provide their customers a solution, affording you the opportunity for a sale for your business as well. Set it up as a regular feature in your e-news: Problem/Solution. Your readers will look forward to each issue. In fact, be sure to include a hyperlink to a page on your site where you archive all of these wonderful cures to their woes! AND provide a comment box where they can submit their questions and problems. This simple step creates that welcome sound of opportunity knocking because you now know their needs and all you have to do is fulfill them.

A third snippet in the e-newsletter may highlight a trend in the industry that you want to encourage your customers to take advantage of to better their business practices. Give them the inside scoop. Provide a blow-by-blow comparison of a new product with something that already exists. If it's something you don't carry (or recommend), show how your alternative fits the bill. If this new trend, product, or service is part of your growing repertoire, add in links to your website where customers can find more information, or better yet, order products and end up at the shopping cart. Adding these links will also help optimize your site with search engines as well.

"Just the facts, ma'am." (DRAGNET)

When you sit down to write your e-news, zoom in on the keywords that get your customers buzzing. Avoid using the word "it" when you can plug a specific item. Put in lots of links to specific pages on your site. When you mention a product by name, build in a hyperlink to its description on your site. And, very important, keep it brief. Keep every entry in your newsletter to a few sentences and end it with "Read more" or "Click here for the full story". These hyperlinks will guide them to your site and, if you are making good use of your tracker, then you will see heightened activity soon after you send your e-news. AND you can see what items have prompted the most interest. Then you know what type of content to include in future issues,

"If you build it, he will come." (FIELD OF DREAMS)

So there's the content, now how do you make the preview look pretty and enticing and send it out without being black-flagged by the SPAM police? There are many content management systems out there that provide templated newsletters. You can adjust color, font size, upload photos, and even personally address the e-newsletter all within the confines of these web-based programs. You will need a subscription for these services and they range in price, some starting as low as $14.95 per month like Constant Contact, where others may cost you thousands of dollars because they are very customized to meet your business' specific needs.

With a beautiful layout chock-full of great content, you're ready to spread the news to the world. Here are a few tips to remember before you hit the "Send" button:

- **ALWAYS have an opt-in and/or opt-out option, ideally at the beginning of the email.** This will prevent your email from being considered SPAM.

- **Respect your customers' privacy.** Let them know upfront, in writing, that the information they give you is private and you will not sell or give it to a third party. Period.

- **Timing is everything.** The best days to send e-marketing messages are Wednesdays and Thursday. Avoid Mondays and Fridays. Look at your web analytics on Tuesdays to determine what you want to promote for the week.

- **More about timing.** Unless you have news about the next trend that is guaranteed to bring home more than a million dollars in one day, consider sending out an e-newsletter every other week. If you consider how many different e-newsletters one person may receive in a day or a week, it can be a bit overwhelming. You want your customers to read your news, not be irritated by the frequency of it and end up hitting the delete button.

- **Keep your content to three "feature" articles that are no longer than a paragraph each.** You want to "tease" your reader and encourage them to click through to your website for more information.

- **Create an "ideas" file of newsworthy items and tidbits you might want to share or write about for later issues.** These will be helpful when you have writer's block and need a little inspiration.

- **Develop an e-newsletter calendar.** Create a plan (go figure) for your e-newsletters, which includes the date that a draft is due, the date of release and what the issue will include. With a written timeline, you'll have a much better chance of making that e-newsletter a reality.

Finally, make sure your e-news complies with the latest CAN-SPAM Act. You must provide a means for the recipient to "unsubscribe" to your newsletter. Check the resources at the end of this book in "A Few Extras" for a link with more details.

An e-newsletter is a great way to get your products and news into your customers' hands quickly, efficiently, and cost-effectively. Make your customers a part of the process and ask them what they want to read and learn more about. All of a sudden, your e-newsletter becomes interactive and you will continue to build your brand into an award-winning, standing-ovation experience.

ACT FIVE ■ An Epic Presentation

"I never knew it could be like this!" **(FROM HERE TO ETERNITY)**

Wow! Just think, you're going to build yourself a web site, make it "live" online because we all know "if you build it, he will come." Right? Not so fast. There's building a website and then there's building a strategy for your online presence. Please don't put the cart before the horse here. While it's exciting to think that your business will have a face in the ominous world of the Web, simply put, you will waste valuable time and hard-earned money just "throwing up" a website. Even worse, you could even do a bit of damage to your "online reputation" by revealing to the search engines that you're not quite on your game. So you need a plan first. Web site second.

As with any successful marketing or business endeavor, you must first think about what you want to accomplish. Set your goals. Then devise a plan on how to achieve them. Think of your business' website as the whole story and each page becomes a scene in that story. One page segues to the next. One prompts action by the viewer or invites the audience to respond. How are you going to lay out the scenes of your story? Where do you want your story to take your audience?

Boy. I got vision and the rest of the world wears bifocals."

(BUTCH CASSIDY AND THE SUNDANCE KID)

Sometimes I hate to even say this, but what may look "beautiful" to you may not dazzle others. First off, make sure that your website — whether it's being designed from scratch or is a revamp of your current site — looks professional. That means clean lines, simple and bold graphics, an easy navigation system, and copy that intrigues but doesn't confuse. You wouldn't show up for a client meeting in flip-flops, cut-off jean shorts, and a T-shirt with a road map of stains. When your customers come to visit you online, they are stepping into your office or your storefront. Find a designer who understands the needs of your business and its customers. Visit competitor web sites and find the ones you like – then find out who designed them or find a qualified designer (one who understands that strategy trumps sweet graphics) and share these URLs. Remember, this is your online professional brand and image. First impressions can make the difference between clicking through to your shopping cart versus being another number in your web analytics' abandon rate.

"Did you ever have the feeling that you wanted to go. and still have the feeling that you wanted to stay?"

(MAN WHO CAME TO DINNER)

What do you want your audience to do while browsing your website? How are you going to keep them engaged long enough to prompt a follow-up sales call or an actual online sales transaction? Are customers learning the latest trends in the industry through informative articles or a newsletter that you've written and posted on your site? Is there a Q & A or FAQ that solves most problems without having to speak with a customer service rep? Does your blog answer questions in real-time or offer insight on new innovations and technology? Is shopping on your site an easy process, right down to the "Checkout" button in your shopping cart? All of the answers to these questions play a huge factor in how you decide to tell your story and set the scenes for each page of the site.

Maybe your site is intended as a stepping stone to encourage customers to visit your physical store or location. If so, you should deeply engage and entice your customers online with insightful information before they visit you. Lead them by the hand so they feel confident they have the knowledge and research to make smart business decisions.

Or, is your web site the actual point of sale? Will your marketing collateral and advertising campaign drive customers to the site to make their purchases? Every page must make a logical contribution to the whole site, contributing to the "big picture". When planning your navigation, ask yourself what you want each particular page to accomplish. Are you informing your visitors of a needed service? Be sure to provide the details of how your approach is distinctive. Do you want to capture information from them? Here's your chance to qualify them with a couple of mouse clicks. It's easy to do if you have dangled the right bait to get them to bite. Is that page trying to close a sale? Map out each page with the desired response from the visitor.

"You talkin' to me? Well I'm the only one here. Who do you think you're talking to?" **(TAXI DRIVER)**

Well, who are you talking to? Do you know? Who is visiting your web site, from where, for how long, and why do they leave? You've got this slick, informative, fantastic, brand spanking new website, but how do you know that it's really working? And when I say "working," I mean, is it delivering the desired results for you, based on the goals you established at the onset of your website plan? There is a slew of ways to track traffic and visitors on your site to determine which pages they are looking at and what keeps them engaged in your site all the way to the final transaction or goal – or where they leave you.

For starters, a site tracker monitors traffic (visitors) on your site. Ideally, you need one that tells you – among other things – where each visitor came from, how long the person remained on your site, the number of pages visited, and which ones. This data indicates where you have strong content that is maintaining reader interest, which pages need to be refined, and how visitors find your site. Analytics programs also provide insight to your site. Many hosts now offer "stats" as part of their hosting package or you can use Google's free analytics (www.google.com/analytics). The free Google reports will show you how you rank against your competition, who is visiting your site, what pages they are visiting, and how often. Once you sign up for this service, you'll see analysis and results immediately. Then you can adjust the "scenes" of your site accordingly.

Great movie scripts sometimes take years to write. I'm not advocating spending that much time on your web site's script, but do take the time to pose thought-provoking questions to yourself and ideas about what you want to accomplish. By developing a truly dynamic and goal-fulfilling site, you will see increase customer loyalty, customer growth and financial results to your bottom line.

ACT SIX ■ Romancing the Audience

"Louis, I think this is the beginning of a beautiful friendship." **(CASABLANCA)**

Relationships. While ultimately we want to close the sale, building relationships is the key to keeping and nurturing long-term customers. So what's your hook, your underlying plot line, that will keep them coming back for more of the story? Because ultimately that's what you want your customers to do, right? Continually come back to you, the Super channel partner. You want to become the end-all, be-all, go-to resource for information, state-of-the-art products and unparalleled service.

Keeping your customers engaged on your website is key, and there are countless creative ways to offer unique online experiences. First, on your site, include the value proposition you use in your other marketing collateral. Do you offer a customized solution? Do you have expertise in a particular area? Whatever it is that sets you apart from the crowd, your website is your platform for telling the world. Your existing customers may know about your specialty, but this is your chance to tell others – those who visited your booth at a trade show but went back home and wondered, "Who are these people and why should I do business with them?" And to those who are getting their first impression of your business from this spot on the World Wide Web.

The next move in your budding love story is your energy, enthusiasm, and desire to please. Continue to write and offer fresh content for your viewers. Written content serves two vital functions. First, it gives visitors a reason to return to see what's new. While it isn't necessary to change your site content daily, make it your directive to regularly add fresh and dynamic articles, ideas, or updates that are meaningful to your visitors. Position yourself as a credible expert who understands their business problems and they will return to your site frequently, eager for more great stuff. The second benefit of fresh content is that search engines like it and use your dynamic commitment to newness as part of their criteria for boosting your page ranking (which is oh so key!). But a word of caution here: Don't rely solely on search engines for bringing customers to your site because their algorithms change frequently and what works one day could be yesterday's news the next.

The next step in nurturing the online relationship with your viewers is to key in to the tech treats that are readily available. Add in some of the new trendy technologies to wow your "TV generation" visitors. Include bonuses like webinars (a teleconference on the Web), podcasts (typically an audio file), and screen capture demonstrations (video files, usually of software applications). These relatively short but powerful images turn browsers into buyers. Or offer a monthly (or at the very least quarterly) newsletter. It's a great way to keep your name in front of customers and prospects. Include a sign-up (opt-in) link on your site, and add their contact information to your database. Consider creating a blog (web log) as an extension of your site, since they are highly favored by search engines. Not sure how to blog? Go to wordpress.com, blogspot.com, or typepad.com to get started.

Lastly, add a shopping cart. Depending on your product or service, site visitors want the ability to buy instantly, so give them that option. If your products lend themselves to being mixed and matched, configure your cart to allow "a la carte" purchases. Finally, be sure the checkout process is simple. The last thing you want is for someone with a full shopping cart to abandon it because checkout took too long — and this happens a lot, so be sure that you have someone else test out your process to be sure you haven't overlooked a glitch.

Bottom line. Entice your visitors to connect with you. Give them a reason to want to come back and watch the next scene unfold. By creating a dynamic story about your business and positioning yourself as a leader and resource in the industry, you will create customers – and sales – for life.

ACT SEVEN ■ Peak Performance

"I'm king of the world!" **(TITANIC)**

So you're feeling pretty darn good about your new website, right? You've written all the story plots for each page, worked closely with a designer who understands your business and your customers, and you're ready to be found on the World Wide Web. Hopefully, in all your excitement of soaring to the top of the Web's "world," you included some great behind-the-scenes search engine optimization work.

Search engine what? Search engine optimization, or SEO, is the set building that will get your website noticed by all the important critics – the search engine crawlers. By using specific keywords in your title tags, meta tags, and text copy on your web pages, these crawlers will search for information about your business and then "rank" you according to how relevant you are to other businesses like yours. Crawlers are the software and technology behind search engines like Google, Yahoo! and MSN. I'll tell you right up front, they will drive you crazy. Once you think you've got them figured out, they change the rules. These all-powerful search engines will force you to stay up-to-date on your website. And if you don't, they'll B-list you pretty quickly. You'll soon be digging deep into the search results to find a reference about your site.

"The question you gotta ask yourself is 'Do I feel lucky?'
Well, do ya, punk?" **(DIRTY HARRY)**

Luck won't get you very far in the search engine world, I'm afraid. Launching a new site without carefully thinking about the words and phrases that customers will use to search for your business is one of the biggest mistakes channel partners can make. You must think like your customers. If they were searching for your products or services, what words would they use in a search engine to find you? Those are the words you need to develop and use on your site.

Create your keywords, or keyterms, before you do anything else. Think of all the words to describe who you are and what you sell, and then some. Identify the search terms that your customers really use and then select those with the highest search volume. Take a look at sites by other channel partners. Google them. See how they rank. Take a look at the highest-ranking site's homepage. Go to the pull-down menu "View" and click on "Source" or "Page Source" and you can actually see your competitor's key words — and get a clue as to why they ranked so high! There are also many research tools available, both free and paid, that can give you hundreds and thousands of keyword combinations, simply by plugging in words that describe who you are. Both Google and Yahoo! have free services; Wordtracker and Keyword Discovery offer more in-depth services for a fee.

After you've developed your list, incorporate these keywords in text on your pages as well as in your web designer's coding. Some hosting companies offer SEO packages with proprietary software that will automatically update your pages with keywords and tags on a regular basis – for a fee, of course. Or you can tap into free resources like Google webmaster tools or Google Analytics to see what pages the crawlers are visiting on your site. Google Analytics will offer you report upon report about your website. These free reports will show you how you rank against your competition, who is visiting your site, what pages they are visiting, and how often. Once you sign up for this service, you'll get analysis and results immediately.

Google Analytics features a "dashboard" that gives you an umbrella overview of the traffic that goes through your website, then various reports that drill down information. Use these reports to determine where your visitors are coming from. Are they putting your URL address right into their web browser or are they finding you with the help of a search engine? If it's via a search engine, you'll learn which one(s) and how often. You may learn that people are "entering" your site through your "Contact Us" page instead of your home page. Why is that? Could your keywords be stronger on that page or your home page? If so, adjust those to garner better page rank for your home page.

You should also consider adding a web tracker to your site's code, which can be done by having your web designer add specific code to the pages you want tracked. Once you choose a tracking program that's right for you, the program will tell you what the code is and where to place it within your website's framework. The great advantage of web trackers is that they are better at tracking "real people" They track browsers, not server requests, and will record your visitors if they return to the same page twice or more. Trackers give you a good inside look at who's visiting your site and how often. All this analysis and tracking information will show you where you're site is garnering results, where's it's not working well, and the areas where you need to make your site perform better.

Great SEO is critical to obtaining high page rankings. Generating sales leads through your website has to be the first step for any company wanting to build an online presence. But if your site cannot be easily found through a search engine, you're probably losing valuable business inquiries every day. Keying in on your keywords is the key to your success.

ENCORE!

*"I didn't come here to tell you how this is going to end.
I came here to tell how it's going to begin."* **(THE MATRIX)**

I don't know about you, but now I'm craving a big bucket of buttered popcorn and a jumbo Diet Coke – all while watching the trailer for your new hit on the Internet!

To say that the World Wide Web is a rapidly changing stage and your website must be dynamic is an understatement. While it helps to understand how the Web and Internet were born, what's now more important than ever is to be at the forefront of how this beast will age – and how your website (your brand!) – will be a visible part of that evolution.

Now that you've completed reading this book, you have the tools to craft the perfect script to cut through the clutter of the hundreds of thousands of websites that exist today. Your website and its placement on the Internet could be the greatest defining aspect of your marketing efforts. It's up to you whether you want to read for the starring role or simply be a walk-on extra. Understand how the Internet works. Allow it to be a dramatic performer in the success of your business so that it's you up there receiving the deafening applause from your customers, not your competitor.

Here are a few tips to keep in mind while writing the award-winning website "script:"

With more than 600 million people worldwide having access to the Web, just think of the audience out there! You may be doing business locally in Akron but there's someone in Beijing who finds you online and wants to "chat" about your products. Don't lose out on this opportunity. Because there is no downtime on the Web, keep your website dynamic and filled with compelling information about your business and your products. With 24/7 access, customers and prospects can find you from anywhere, an opportunity that could easily be missed if your website contains outdated or miscellaneous information that's not very useful.

Know your search engines and how they operate. This insight is critical to the success of your website and brand. By updating your site frequently and keeping the content dynamic and ever-changing, you will garner higher rankings with search engines like Google, Yahoo! and MSN (the big three). These critics will make or break you when it comes to website rankings. By learning what each search engine requires in order to be "seen" by its crawlers, you have the ability to manipulate your information so that the crawler pays attention to you! It's kind of like having the inside line on the characteristics a director needs for his lead actor. You have a much better chance of landing the role – or the customer in your case.

Consider having a Facebook, MySpace, LinkedIn, or other social networking existence on the Web. This stuff is not just for kids, folks. Gone are the days of Chamber mixers once a month (where the same crowd gathers, shaking the same hands, and pitching the same deal every time). Being involved in social networking allows you to connect to all sorts of an unlimited number of groups, be it of like interest, location, age, whatever. These online communities can trigger a chain of events that can lead to new customers from sources you never imagined! They're casual, easy to use, and free! And who doesn't love to socialize?

Plan, plan, plan. Create a strategy and an outline for your website before you spend thousands of dollars having your metro-area's top designer build it. By understanding what your goals are for your site before you build it, you'll have a clear vision of what needs to happen on the site, where entry points should be, whether or not to have a shopping cart, and how to include data collection. See where I'm going here? There are lots of aspects that you must consider about how your online business is going to work. All the bells and whistles in the world won't prompt a customer to click through to "Checkout" if the path to get them there is cumbersome. Write your script first, then make it functional and pretty.

Ultimately you want your customers to keep coming back to your site to buy more, more, more. But in order to do that, you must give them something in return. Yes, you're going to give away something but it really won't cost you much, if anything at all. While you want your customers to click "Order Now", your customers want to feel like they have gained something by being on your site. Podcasts, blogs, e-newsletters, and other digital communications are a great way to give your customers information and tools about new trends, helpful hints, ways to troubleshoot, and insider information. Your real goal here is to build long-term relationships with customers so they keep coming back to you for their needs, not to your competitors. Give a little. It will go a long way.

Always remember that the World Wide Web is constantly changing and this year's award-winner may be next year's B-lister. Stay up with the latest trends and constantly feed your site with new information that will be helpful and beneficial to your customers. Give them a reason to keep coming back for encore after encore. After all, a really great movie deserves to be viewed more than once.

A Few Extras!

"Life moves pretty fast. If you don't stop and look around once in awhile. you could miss it" **(FERRIS BUELLER'S DAY OFF)**

SEARCH ENGINES

ABOUT SEARCH ENGINES: About.com has a good directory of information about the all-powerful search engines, from the hundreds of smaller niche ones to the Big Three (Google, Yahoo, MSN).

GOOGLE BUSINESS SOLUTIONS: Get more from this powerful search engine than just lists of results. Learn how to make it work for your business, with Google Analytics, AdWords, and more.

YAHOO BUZZ: A great place to search trends: what's hot now and what's heating up.

REGISTER YOUR URL

If you haven't already purchased your domain name (URL), here are a few places to go where you can search to see if the name is available and then buy what you want, including hosting:

NETWORK SOLUTIONS

GODADDY

BLOGGING

Blogging is red hot right now. And it's easy to get started. Check out these blog hosts; some are free and others charge. You decide what works best for you!

BLOGGER

TYPEPAD

WORDPRESS

KEYWORDS

Find the right keywords to help people find you via the search engines with these research tools:

KEYWORDDISCOVERY

WORDTRACKER

VIDEO

YOUTUBE: THE place to be seen online! Upload a video here and harness the viral power of the Internet.

SOCIAL NETWORKS

MYSPACE: One of the top social media networks on the planet.

FACEBOOK: Ditto!

LINKEDIN: Connect with professionals on this business network.

SPAM RULES

FEDERAL TRADE COMMISSION: The best email campaign can fail if you haven't followed the SPAM rules!

Author! Author!

A dedicated marketing professional, Michelle Kabele has been helping technology companies develop award-winning channel partner programs and marketing strategies for over 10 years. Her innovative channel marketing concepts have been adopted and implemented by many leading technology companies, including Zebra Technologies, 3Com Corporation and U.S. Robotics. Moreover, Michelle has worked extensively with channel partners throughout North America and thoroughly understands the realities and practicalities they face in planning and executing effective promotional, marketing, and sales campaigns.

Michelle has an MBA from the J.L. Kellogg Graduate School of Management (Evanston, IL) and an undergraduate degree from Northwestern University (Evanston, IL).

For more great ways to build your business,
check out Michelle Kabele's other books:

Great Marketing Is Free!

50 Easy Ideas for Improving Your Business

Just Say "Yes!": The Power of Creative Thinking Outside That Tired Old Box

Visit **www.ideastormpress.com** for the most up-to-the-minute news,
advice, ideas, and just cool stuff.

www.ingramcontent.com/pod-product-compliance
Lightning Source LLC
Chambersburg PA
CBHW071412200326
41520CB00014B/3410